Ahead of Their Time

Pioneers Who Seized Tomorrow, Today

Lynn Miller

Net worlding PUBLISHING

ISBN: 978-1-959993-47-6

Contents

Introduction
Seeing What's Already True

All thirteen pioneers figured out the same thing: being ahead of your time doesn't happen because you create something new. It happens when you spot something everyone else misses. You see a possibility and act even when you're not sure it'll work.

Right now, something is driving you crazy. A process that wastes time. A problem everyone complains about but accepts. A better way that nobody will try. That frustration? It's actually telling you something important. You're seeing what everyone else has given up noticing.

After conducting over 200 hours of interviews, I discovered each pioneer's story started the same way: they were annoyed by something fixable that everyone else had given up on. They didn't set out to change the world. They couldn't stand watching solvable problems stay broken. Over time, their personal frustrations became solutions that helped thousands of people.

What makes them different? They see obstacles as opportunities and view progress as small steps rather than giant leaps. Most importantly, they act on what they see instead of just complaining about it.

The difference comes down to one thing: they ask different questions. While most people ask 'How can I succeed?' pioneers ask 'How can I help everyone succeed?' That shift changes everything.

The pioneer highlighted in each chapter tells a story about how they found a unique way to turn frustration into opportunity. You'll see their breakthrough moments, who helped them along the way, decisions they made when challenges arose, and discover what you can do with what you already know.

Part One
How Pioneers Think Differently

The three pioneers in chapters 1 through 3 figured out the same thing: the way everyone else thinks about problems is different.

Every time someone said 'that's impossible,' Leanne Gordon asked 'What if there's another way?' Her clients broke through years of gridlock with that single question.

Rabbi Debra Newman-Kamin built her entire teaching approach around one challenge: "

"How do you know?" Instead of asking people to accept answers on faith, she shows them how to find rock-solid sources for their beliefs.

Henna Pryor discovered the awkwardness she'd been trying to fix her whole life was actually valuable data. While others competed in crowded markets, she built a business around the emotion everyone feels but nobody talks about.

Each pioneer exemplifies a distinct thinking pattern you can adopt.

Chapter 1
Leanne Gordon: The Power of "What If"

Leanne Gordon always challenged the clients to ask her more unexpected questions. Not polite questions that keep conversations pleasant but the kind that make people shift in their seats and crack open possibilities no one had considered.

Working as a young professional in Perth, Australia, Leanne noticed something: "I don't get enough questions," she reflects. "There's always this interesting relationship with questions in both life and work." Leanne's hunger for deeper inquiry became the foundation of how she approaches organizational change.

Leanne landed her first job at Clough, an Australian engineering company. Fresh out of university in the early 1990s, she had no idea she'd stumbled into something special.

"Harold Clough was a visionary," Gordon explains. "He saw things differently and was a natural people leader. And, he was uncharacteristically intuitive, which goes against the stereotype of an engineer. When I worked with Harold, I realized my purpose: to work with people and bring mutually beneficial employer-employee experiences to their work."

The Challenge of Being Different

When Leanne later moved to other organizations, she hit a wall of traditional thinking where workplace cultures forgot about humans entirely.

"It can be lonely when you think you're the only one with a specific set of ideas," she admits. "Harold helped me see that my purpose was showing people how organizing and working differently impacts their ability to work together."

Working as a change agent in traditional organizations, Gordon consistently found herself thinking steps ahead of everyone else.

"Sometimes I feel like I arrived on a different planet," she admits. "I found myself constantly challenged by the ideas I bring or how I draw from multiple fields to create new solutions. People say, 'What's that got to do with it?' I say, 'Well, it's similar when you line it up.'"

Gordon reads everything. Some of her favorite topics include economics, philosophy, and psychology. "That holistic approach to seeing any problem from several different perspectives is one attribute that makes me different."

At the heart of Gordon's approach is the belief that success doesn't have to come at anyone's expense.

"Company success doesn't have to come at the expense of the people doing the work," she explains. When companies ask her, "Why do we lose people? Why can't we get people engaged?" she knows the answer: put people at the heart of the organization.

"When we put people at the heart of an organization, we open up the possibility of success."

The Power of "What If"

Gordon's most potent tool is deceptively simple: two words that shift entire conversations.

"I offer people another way of looking at situations by asking, 'What if this were possible?'" she explains. "I like to come at the problem by focusing on a connected idea they hadn't considered."

Unlike yes-or-no questions that shut down conversation, "what if" questions invite exploration. They shift thinking from limitations to possibilities.

Finding Your Tribe

Leanne's experience living in one of the world's most remote cities, where she thought differently from everyone around her, created profound isolation.

"Anyone who thinks outside the middle of the curve feels like they're on the outer edge," she shares. "You feel like your ideas come from a different planet."

The breakthrough came through Seth Godin's altMBA program, where she discovered what Godin calls "people like us."

"When I work inside organizations, it feels like a different game. I enjoy connecting with people who are more in sync with the game I prefer to play."

When asked about her most important lesson, Gordon talks about self-trust.

"People say, 'I'm not comfortable with change.' My response is, 'You live through different every day.' The weather changes. You see an accident on your commute and take a different route. You don't say, 'Oh no, I'm scared of changing.' We're constantly adapting, but we've convinced ourselves we're not good at it."

Gordon helps people recognize their natural adaptability. "When you draw on the comfort that you've made change before, initiating and adapting to change becomes possible."

The Current Moment

After 30 years of work in organizational change, Leanne Gordon sees both progress and regression.

"People in organizations resist change," she observes. "There's a regression which feels like the walls are closing in. People say, 'We've seen what's possible, and we don't like it.'"

Leanne's work now focuses on individual coaching, particularly with women "trying to do something different and jump out" from traditional career paths.

What This Means for You

Leanne Gordon proves that pioneering often begins with two simple words: "What if?"

Her journey from a young professional hungry for more profound questions to a change agent who transforms organizations reveals a truth: The questions others avoid are often the ones that unlock everything.

Every limitation you face is a starting point. Every time you tell yourself "that's just how things are," stop and think of this moment as an invitation to ask "What if there's a different way?"

Gordon's win-win philosophy shows that success doesn't require someone else to lose. When you put people at the heart of any system, you change what's possible.

The next time someone tells you what you want can't be done, remember Leanne Gordon in Perth, asking the questions that make people shift in their seats. Then ask your own "what if" and watch what opens up.

What if the problem everyone agrees is "impossible" to solve in your situation is the most critical question to explore?

The power of questioning everything extends beyond business strategy. As we'll see in the next chapter, Rabbi Debra Newman-Kamin discovered that the simple question "How do you know?" transformed not just her leadership style, but her entire congregation's approach to faith and community.

Chapter 2
"How Do You Know?"

When the Rabbi of Am Yisrael in Northfield, Illinois, Debra Newman-Kamin, heard these four words from a skeptical teenager, something clicked. Not because she had a perfect answer, but because she realized this question could shape her leadership.

"I hear the teenager's voice: 'How do you know?'" she explains. "The challenge from students who wouldn't accept anything at face value became the foundation of everything I did as a rabbi."

She knew it wasn't about undermining authority; instead, Newman-Kamin used this question as a way of building on solid ground.

Most religious leaders bristle when people constantly question them. Newman-Kamin embraced it. "How do you know?" forced her to do something radical: cite her sources. Every teaching, every decision, every piece of advice had to come from something verifiable, not just her opinion.

"Sometimes I have to say things that upset people," Newman-Kamin acknowledges, whether we discuss keeping kosher or difficult life situations. "What motivates me isn't kindness itself. I'm motivated by kindness as part of this framework of tradition."

Breaking Ground Without Trying

Rabbi Newman-Kamin joined the second class of female rabbis in the Conservative movement, though that was not her plan. As a college student of Judaic studies, she felt drawn to Jewish community work but hadn't considered the rabbinate until she met Rabbi Ellen Dreyfus while babysitting.

"She was the first person who said to me, 'Why don't you think about becoming a rabbi?' That was mind-blowing because I always thought of rabbis as very observant men."

While she was studying in Israel, the Conservative movement of Judaism made the historic decision to ordain women. "If I'd been born 10 years earlier, I would have been deep in my career and this type of opportunity was not available. So much of my life was just being in the right place at the right time."

Newman-Kamin entered a class with over 30 students, half of whom were women. "There was a backlog of women waiting to get into rabbinical school," she explains. This critical mass provided support that might not have existed otherwise.

Still, the challenges were real. "There were professors who adamantly opposed accepting women into rabbinical school. I felt like I had to work twice as hard as all the men. The professors were sure I would not have the right answer."

After graduating from rabbinical school, Newman-Kamin faced a choice between a position with the Jewish student group, Hillel, at the University of Chicago and an assistant rabbi position at Am Yisrael. The chance to work with Rabbi Harold Frankel proved irresistible.

"Rabbi Frankel was so special. He was an established rabbi who left another pulpit to start Am Yisrael, and was an outspoken advocate for civil rights.

As Rabbi Frankel got older, he knew he wanted to hire a female rabbi that he could mentor to be his successor.

Newman-Kamin, who lived in the Chicago area, was his choice."

"I didn't think I had anything to offer in a pulpit position. I didn't think I knew enough. After meeting with Rabbi Frankel, I did not meet with anyone else. It was his decision, and that was huge, because women getting through search committees in a conservative synagogue was almost impossible then."

What she thought would be a three-to-five-year mentorship became her entire career.

Early in her career as an assistant rabbi, Newman-Kamin's began working with the Rabbinical Assembly. She helped create opportunities for other women in the rabbinate and eventually became the first female president of the Rabbinical Assembly.

"The timing made it possible for opportunities that sort of fell in my lap. I've had men at every stage of my career holding the door open for me, and I paid it forward."

Building Community Through Real Relationships

Under Newman-Kamin's leadership, Am Yisrael became known for something beyond traditional synagogue metrics: authentic community.

"Everything in Judaism happens in community. Adding specific types of music during certain sections of the service was another change that involved the community. If you're not building a community of people, if you're not helping create relationships, you don't have a meaningful congregation.

The COVID-19 pandemic tested this belief. People could access quality religious content from anywhere, yet life cycle events revealed what was missing. "When it came time to be a mourner, they wanted to be surrounded by people. The same thing happened with getting married—many weddings were postponed. Nobody wants to do their wedding alone in their backyard."

During the pandemic, Newman-Kamin introduced innovative methods for people attending Bar and Bat Mitzvahs, along with other life-cycle events.

For Bar and Bat Mitzvahs, protective shields were installed in front of where the speakers stood, and a limited number of people were invited to the synagogue, sitting socially distant.

Over time, the Bar and Bat Mitzvah children were allowed to read from the torah while at home via Zoom and services were live-streamed.

Eventually, the congregation was allowed to return to synagogue, required to wear masks, and socialized outside whenever possible.

When long-term staff members retired, Newman-Kamin acknowledged the difficulty while recognizing growth potential.

"I see the potential in all this change. The change isn't easy. But I can see the potential for good in it, not just the loss."

Seeing potential during change keeps Am Yisrael nimble. "We move very quickly. That's not really because of me. It's because of the nature of the congregation. Fortunately, I feel most comfortable working quickly when our congregation needs to face change."

Newman-Kamin's question, "How do you know?" reveals something powerful: authority comes from intellectual humility, not assumed expertise. By welcoming questions rather than deflecting them, this Chicago-based rabbi continues to build a legacy on solid ground rather than shifting sand.

We spoke briefly about the future of women in the rabbinate. "Acceptance of women rabbis will continue to grow. As information becomes more abundant and questionable, leaders who thrive will be those who can say exactly how they know what they know."

Newman-Kamin's approach to leadership reminds us that stating the facts doesn't work-cite your sources. Don't assume authority; build it through evidence.

Advice for Future Pioneers

Turn disruption into opportunity. When change hits your organization, acknowledge the loss while articulating what's possible. Help your team see potential in transitions that terrify them. Your ability to navigate uncertainty with confidence will determine whether people follow you through change or resist it.

Newman-Kamin's "How do you know?" reveals your secret weapon: intellectual humility beats assumed expertise every time. Welcome the hard questions. Chase down the sources. Build your leadership on evidence, not ego.

When asked for advice to other leaders, Newman-Kamin's response is direct: "Just tell the story."

"Everything doesn't have to be over-explained. Just tell the story. Answer the question, 'What are we doing here?'"

Master the art of story. As attention spans shrink and complexity increases, leaders who distill complex ideas into compelling narratives will outperform those who believe, "that's just the way it is."

That teenager who challenged Rabbi Newman-Kamin had no idea those four words would transform her entire approach to leadership. Your most powerful breakthroughs often arrive disguised as your most uncomfortable moments.

Speaking of uncomfortable moments, what happens when your questions make people feel awkward? When does the room go silent? When someone says, "Nobody's ever asked that before."

Pay attention. That discomfort is data.

In our next chapter, executive coach Henna Pryor shows you why these awkward moments aren't problems to avoid-they're signals you're onto something important. She built a successful consulting business (and wrote a book) on the very feeling everyone else tries to eliminate. She calls it "Good Awkward," and it might be the most valuable skill you're not developing.

Chapter 3
Why the Front Door is Overrated

While the $366 billion professional development industry obsesses over confidence training, Henna Pryor discovered something that contradicts everything we think we know about workplace success: 84% of working Americans say social skills are crucial for navigating change at work, yet 30% would rather clean a toilet than ask a coworker for help.

"That's not just ironic," Henna explains. "It's dangerous."

The numbers get worse. Her research found that 56% of workers prefer working alone rather than with colleagues, despite knowing that collaboration is important. Companies like Johnson & Johnson and Astra-

Zeneca spend millions on teamwork training, yet their employees actively avoid each other.

"I spoke at conferences for these companies, and they all complained: our people work in silos. They don't communicate across departments."

Everyone else keeps chasing similar tired solutions, such as more confidence training, another vulnerability workshop, and one more courage seminar. Henna went the opposite direction. She found her opportunity in the very thing everyone was trying to eliminate: awkwardness.

Seizing the opportunity to lean into awkwardness was what Henna calls "finding the side door."

"I always say it's fine to go through the front door. But when your goal is to be ahead of your time, you have to find the side doors. The front door is very crowded. There's a line there."

From Immigrant's Daughter to Side Door Expert

Most success stories start with privilege. Henna's began with exclusion.

Henna was the firstborn daughter of immigrants. She

spent her childhood acutely aware of how she stood out when all she wanted was to fit in.

"I didn't feel pretty. I didn't feel like my clothes were the same. I didn't think my food smelled the same as the other kids' in the cafeteria. I constantly felt different when all I wanted to do was fit in."

Here's what nobody tells you about feeling like an outsider: it trains you to see what insiders miss. Each professional breakthrough Henna experienced brought back those old, awkward feelings. "Every time I reached an inflection point where I had a chance to do something significant, feeling awkward came rushing back."

Most people would have spent years in therapy trying to eliminate this feeling. Henna did something radically different and followed it.

The turning point came while reading Brené Brown's tagline: "Stay brave, kind, and awkward."

"Stay brave? Yes, I know that one. Stay kind? My parents taught me that. But stay awkward? No, thank you. I've tried to get rid of this feeling for years."

That resistance turned out to be Henna's first clue. She began to wonder if the things we resist most vehemently often become our most fulfilling opportunities.

Then she stumbled on a question from executive coach Jerry Colonna that flipped everything: "How are you complicit in creating the conditions you say you don't want?"

The question caused Henna to take a step back. "I can sit there and say, I have too much work on my plate. Instead, I try to stop and ask myself periodically: How are you complicit, Henna, in creating the conditions you say you don't want?"

While everyone else was trying to become less awkward, Henna realized something different: awkwardness isn't a character flaw. It's intelligence.

"There's no such thing as a factually awkward person," she explains. "Awkwardness is an emotion. It is a state, not a trait."

Think about that. Every time a client says they're "too awkward" to give presentations, they're creating the exact limitation they claim to hate. The identity box becomes the prison.

The Strengths Trap Everyone Falls Into

Here's the sacred cow Henna slaughters: "Lean into your strengths."

"I take issue with the overemphasis on leaning into our strengths. We should use our strengths situationally. But too much of that narrative goes too far."

She gets specific about why this "trap" keeps people stuck: "Suppose you're an aspiring executive woman in middle management looking to move into senior ranks, and you're an excellent researcher and writer but not great at commanding a room. I don't want you to lean into your strengths. I want you to stop doing that entirely, for a while. Commanding a room is your new priority."

The strength obsession nearly cost Henna everything; she didn't focus on what she could do. "If I focused only on the strengths I knew I had, I would have left behind the ones I didn't know I had. I didn't know I would be a good book writer."

So how did she go from a $250 speaking fee in November 2021 to commanding keynote rates? Not through some grand strategy. Through small bets that most people are too proud to make.

"Place small bets constantly. When you place small bets, it allows you to seed an idea and see if there are legs. If it doesn't work out, it was a small bet. Not that big a deal."

She's failed more than she's succeeded. "I have so many small bets that failed. Guess who knows about them? The three people who saw it when it happened."

The difference? She kept placing small bets while others kept planning.

How Small Bets Actually Work

Here's how Henna describes what small bets look like in practice: "Before I launch a group program, I test the approach with an existing executive coaching client first. Before I write a new book, I start by sharing the idea in LinkedIn posts."

Henna explains the pattern is simple: she finds small ways to pressure test ideas before making large investments. A few LinkedIn posts show whether people care about a topic. No market research. No focus groups. Just honest feedback from real people.

"Finding small viable ways to pressure test ideas before going all in works well. I used the same approach for the two LinkedIn courses I offer.

The beauty of this approach? When ideas fail, they fail small. When they work, Henna already knows there's demand before she builds anything big.

What's Coming Next

Forget what the trend reports tell you. Henna sees three shifts that will blindside everyone who's still fighting at the front door:

Social Skills Will Become Premium Currency.

"As AI handles more technical work, the ability to navigate awkward conversations, build genuine relationships, and collaborate effectively will become the ultimate differentiator." Translation: The thing everyone's avoiding will become the thing everyone needs.

The Awkwardness Advantage Will Go Mainstream. "Within five years, you'll see 'awkwardness training' alongside confidence training." The companies spending millions to eliminate awkwardness will start spending millions to cultivate it.

Side Door Thinking Will Replace Linear Career Planning. "The traditional career ladder is dead. The future belongs to people who can spot opportunities in overlooked spaces." While your colleagues polish their resumes for the same promotions, you'll be creating positions that don't exist yet.

Henna isn't trying to motivate you. She applied pattern recognition skills acquired during her two and a half years in Big Four accounting, and prioritized freedom over her parents' definition of success.

"I realized that I'm not afraid to get it wrong. But don't tell me I can't try."

Lessons to Learn: Your Side Door Is Waiting

Don't let the identity box become your prison. The opportunity isn't in becoming more confident, more polished, or more like everyone else. It's in the thing you're trying to hide.

When a conversation gets awkward, when people shift in their seats, when someone says "That's interesting, but..." everyone else backs off. That's precisely when you should lean in.

Most people treat discomfort like a stop sign. Pioneers treat it like a map. That stomach-drop moment in a meeting? That's not telling you to keep quiet. It's telling you you're onto something.

Challenge the truths no one questions. Even the positive ones. Especially the positive ones. What unique capabilities in your field have you never examined? That blind spot might be someone's billion-dollar business.

Stop focusing on why know how, that awkwardness,

your discomfort, your weird perspective doesn't quite fit? That's not your weakness. That's your side door.

The question isn't whether you'll use it. The question is whether you'll use it before everyone else figures out it exists. What would happen if the side door presents challenges? Learn more about people who stepped up to this challenge in Part Two: Turning Problems into opportunities.

Part Two
Turning Problems Into Opportunities

Ever wonder what happens when someone finally gets fed up enough to do something about it?

Dr. Tenia Davis got tired of being excluded from meetings while watching her toxic boss give everyone else advance notice. She carried two coffee cups into his office and had the conversation that changed her career. It taught her that most "problem employees" are just good people stuck in broken systems.

Andy Crestodina watched businesses fail from terrible marketing advice and decided to give away his best secrets for free. While competitors called him crazy, his "teaching beats selling" approach built one of Chicago's most respected agencies.

Loren Williams saw the digital divide keeping entire communities behind and used his tech background to bridge gaps that others ignored. He proved that the best business opportunities often come from solving problems that affect people who can't afford typical solutions.

You'll see how each pioneer turned personal frustration into solutions that helped thousands of others facing the same problems.

Chapter 4
When Good Employees Go Bad

D
r. Tenia Davis carried two cups of coffee into what would become the most important conversation of her career. One for herself, one for the boss who had spent months leaving her out of meetings, sending her invitations at the last minute while giving others days of notice, and hosting team lunches without her because, as he put it, "they would talk about things she wasn't interested in."

"I love what I'm doing," she told him that morning, her voice steady despite her racing heart. "I'm pretty good at it, and I'm learning a lot from this team. I don't want to leave the team, but I need you to be the leader that I respect."

The words surprised even her. She hadn't planned to say them, but there they were, hanging in the air between two coffee cups and years of frustration. Her supervisor looked shocked. Tenia felt surprised by saying it. But in that moment of unscripted honesty, something clicked.

"I had nothing to lose," she reflects now. "Sometimes you have to risk everything to find out what you're truly capable of."

Companies spend $87 billion annually trying to fix "problem employees," but Tenia discovered they're solving the wrong problem. Gallup research shows that managers account for 70% of employee engagement issues. The managers create the problems they think they're solving.

"I kept seeing the same pattern," Tenia explains. "Great employees would come in motivated and excited, then six months later they'd be disengaged, doing the bare minimum, or looking for the exit. Everyone blamed the employees. I started to start looking at the environment."

During this time, Tenia became the problem employee.

That coffee conversation didn't come from nowhere. Tenia spent months wrestling with a question many ambitious people face: When does persistence become self-sabotage? Her inner voice kept warning her about the toxic culture, but she kept pushing through, telling herself it was just a job. The conflicts around her grew worse. Something inside her knew when work felt right; when she contributed something meaningful. This wasn't it.

So Tenia took action. She researched her supervisor, printed his bio, and highlighted the skills she wanted to learn in yellow. She brought that paper to their coffee meeting. "You're brilliant. You're smart. That's why I'm here. I want to learn from you," she told him. "But you're not creating a way for me to learn from you, and I feel like I'm getting the raw end of the deal."

She didn't threaten or insult. She spoke from respect and genuine desire to learn, but she also drew a line: "Enough. I'm not going anywhere. I want to learn, and I want to learn it here."

The risk paid off. Tenia completed the project, finished her training, and found other mentors within the organization who supported her growth. More importantly, the experience taught her how to have difficult conversations without burning bridges. She learned to craft her words so people could hear hard truths without feeling attacked.

But Tenia also learned when persistence becomes harmful. "I'm a fixer," she explains. "Typically, I go into an organization to fix things. But sometimes it's okay to fix and go. Sometimes staying is not in your best interest."

This lesson hit home during her time in HR, when her job became laying people off. One day she encountered someone she'd laid off, now begging for money on the street. The person wasn't a bad employee—the department had dissolved, and the employee Tenia laid off built their entire career in one place. They didn't know anything else.

"I do not want that job anymore," Tenia decided. "I just don't want to do that."

At 58, Tenia redefined what thriving meant. For some, it means making lots of money and climbing ladders. For her, it means doing passionate work with people who share her values, building something that matters, leaving a legacy. "At 58, how many toys can you have? Making lots of money just doesn't cut it."

Her new definition of success includes learning from anyone. She remembers when a CEO partnered executives with IT interns as technology emerged. While her peers bristled at taking direction from twenty-somethings, Tenia said, "Bring it on. Teach me what you know." She gained respect from a different generation and learned things that fast-tracked her career. "Wow, I can do that with one click. Are you serious?"

This openness extends to how she thinks about breaking rules. Rule-breaking isn't just about having guts—it's knowing when and how to challenge norms effectively.

Her advice: "Put yourself in an environment at least once a week that is foreign to you. Life is constant change, and if you only deal with change when others bring it to you, then you don't know how to deal with change in different settings."

Through all these experiences, Tenia identified three critical capabilities for leading change: self-awareness, adaptability, and curiosity. "I'm not afraid to fail, and I'm not afraid to say I'm wrong. People who are more self-directed and open to seeking knowledge tend to evolve."

Her story leads to three questions to ask yourself that could change how you see your own workplace challenges:

Three Questions That Change Everything

Question 1: What if the problem isn't the person? Before you label someone as difficult or lazy, examine their environment. Do they get excluded from essential conversations? Do they receive meeting invites at the last minute while others receive days of advance notice? Do they have the same learning opportunities as everyone else?

Most "problem employees" are capable people stuck in broken systems.

Question 2: Am I staying to grow or staying because I'm scared? Tenia learned the difference between functional persistence and harmful stubbornness. Sometimes the most professional thing you can do is leave a situation that's not working, even when you're good at your job.

Question 3: Is this place helping me become better, or am I just comfortable being miserable?

When Tenia confronted her boss, she didn't lead with complaints. She led with contribution: "You're brilliant. That's why I'm here. But you're not creating a way for me to thrive." She focused on what she wanted to contribute rather than what was wrong with him. That's why the conversation worked instead of backfiring.

If you're a manager, stop assuming struggling employees are the problem. Look at what's happening around them. If you're the struggling employee, trust that inner voice telling you something's wrong. You're probably not the problem, but you need to decide: Will you speak up like Tenia, find other mentors, or recognize it's time to go?

The question isn't whether you're brave enough to speak up or smart enough to leave. It's whether you're ready to stop accepting conditions that prevent you and those around you from doing your best work.

It took courage for Tenia to say what needed to be said. But what happens when you discover that giving away your best ideas for free is the most innovative business move you can make?

Andy Crestodina build his well-known company, Orbit Media, by teaching instead of selling, proving that generosity can be the ultimate competitive advantage.

Chapter 5
"The Generosity Contest"

D espite 70% of companies investing in content marketing, only 30% consider it effective. Andy Crestodina figured out what the other 70% are getting wrong: they're trying to sell instead of serve.

"Most marketing feels like someone trying to sell you something," Andy explains. "People smell that from a mile away. But what if marketing were helpful? What if instead of trying to get attention, you earned trust by teaching people something useful?"

Andy discovered finding creative ways to keep earning trust interesting: "I thought, wow, I can enter this contest of generosity to be the most helpful, useful internet citizen possible. The most successful content marketers are simply the most generous people on the internet."

The Art-Science Sweet Spot

Andy walked away from a high-paying recruiting job to start Orbit Media for one reason: "I always wanted to do a job that uses both halves of my brain. Digital marketing combines art and science. It combines the creative and technical. It combines analytics with design."

Everywhere he looked, Andy saw the same problem. Designers created stunning websites that didn't convert. Tech people built functional tools that felt cold and life-less. Nobody was bridging the gap.

"I wanted to live in that space where art meets science, and I would do anything to make it happen. I quit my recruiting job, despite it paying well, because I didn't enjoy it. I cared more about building something new than I cared about money."

The result? Orbit Media's websites don't just win design awards—they generate 47% higher conversion rates than the industry average. His clients include Coyote Logistics (sold to UPS for $1.8 billion), Work-front Software (acquired for $1.5 billion), and dozens of B2B companies that doubled their leads within 18 months.

Andy doesn't take just any client. He chooses to work with companies that demonstrate empathy in how they treat employees, customers, and the environment. This led to the company by becoming a Certified B Corp over 10 years ago.

"I try to look at the world from the perspective of the buyer," he says. When Andy helps these companies improve their business, it creates better cultures and stronger employee relationships. The values alignment matters more than the contract size.

While competitors blast "We're #1!" messages, Andy helps visitors figure out if they're in the right place. "Making your writing specific enough so that the right person says, 'Ah, this is perfect for me,' and the wrong person says, 'Ah, I'm in the wrong place.'"

This approach generates 60% fewer leads but 3x higher close rates. The people who contact Orbit already know they want to work together.

Teaching Content Marketing to 281,000 People at Once

Most agencies guard their methods like state secrets. Andy distributes digital marketing tips to 265,000 LinkedIn newsletter subscribers weekly along with another group of 16,000+ subscribers looking for web marketing tips every two weeks.

"I never wanted to keep secrets. Early on in my business, I made it my mission to share valuable insights on the internet."

His newsletters don't waste time with theory. They deliver specific how-tos, such as: Increase email open rates by 23% with this subject line formula and, which headline structure generates 2x more clicks? Readers want to implement these techniques immediately—some do it themselves, others hire Orbit to execute.

Not to generate leads, but to elevate everyone's work. "Teachers try to make a difference in someone's life. Marketers try to persuade you to take action. At our best, we're trying to make a difference in the world."

People who follow Andy notice something unusual: he gives away information that other agencies charge thousands to access. No strings attached. No expectations. He wants to leave a legacy of marketers who know how to help rather than manipulate.

The numbers prove this works. Orbit Media gets 76% of new business from referrals—triple the agency average. When he launches a new service, it sells out before he advertises it.

The AI Advantage Nobody Sees

While everyone uses AI to write faster, Andy uses it to think better.

"I strongly believe that the most popular use case for AI, writing things, is the least interesting and useful. The most effective use of AI is making something better, finding gaps, and auditing what you're already working on."

Instead of asking AI to write marketing copy, he trains it to become his ideal customer. "I train the AI to act like my ideal customer. I talk about their hopes, fears, what triggers them emotionally, and how they make decisions. Then I show the AI my website or article and ask, 'What do you think?'"

This virtual focus group caught problems that cost competitors thousands in lost conversions. One client's homepage had a subtle disconnect between headline and hero image that Andy's AI customer spotted immediately. Fixing it increased conversions by 31%.

Andy sees what's coming: "Years from now, instead of opening a browser and going to Google, people will just open their AI app and ask, 'Who's the best person for this?'"

While competitors wait to see what happens, Orbit Media has already fed AI systems 1,200 case studies, 500 detailed tutorials, and performance data from 2,000 websites. When someone asks AI for the best web design agency in Chicago, guess whose name comes up first?

The Payback of Generosity

On the day of our interview, Andy flew to Boston to teach a seven-hour workshop on AI and digital marketing. He won't pitch anything. He won't collect leads. He'll just teach.

"I don't need to come back with a lead. All I'm doing is trying to help people do their job better. If my help changes how they work, they'll remember me."

Critics call this naive. The results say otherwise. A workshop attendee from 2019 just signed a six-figure contract. Someone Andy helped with a quick LinkedIn message in 2021 referred three large clients. His free webinar series generated $2.3 million in revenue from people who attended, learned something useful, then hired Orbit months or years later.

"People think I'm foolish for not having a better filter. Why would I agree to this interview? There's no obvious benefit to me. But it doesn't matter. I get to meet someone. I'm enjoying this conversation."

After returning from Boston, Andy shared one final insight: "I don't really understand something until I've taught it. Organizing my thoughts around a concept isn't complete until it's explained out loud to a group. Teaching is the final step in learning. A concept isn't fully grasped until it's handed off to someone else."

Your Contest Begins Now

Pick one piece of knowledge that could help someone in your field. Not a sales pitch disguised as advice. Real, actionable information they can use today.

Share it publicly this week. Don't gate it behind an email form. Don't save the best part for paying clients. Give away the thing that makes you valuable.

Andy's formula works because it's simple: "Always meet new people, and always do good work. Just do those two things, and somehow it will work out."

The internet's contest of generosity has one rule: whoever helps the most people wins. While your competitors hoard their secrets, you could be building an army of people who trust you because you've already helped them succeed.

The most successful people on the internet aren't the smartest or the loudest. They're the ones who gave value before anyone asked to buy it.

Chapter 6
Closing the Digital Divide

Loren Williams was watching TV when his life changed. Not through a movie or the news, but Governor Pritzker's daily COVID briefing. Boring stuff, usually. But that day in 2020, the governor said something that made Loren sit up straight.

"We're telling people to work from home, go to school online, use Telehealth," Pritzker said. "But there are over a million families in Illinois who can't do any of that. They don't have a computer or internet. We're leaving 1.1 million families behind."

Then, Pritzker mentioned bringing a nonprofit called PCs for People to Illinois. Loren had never heard of them, but something clicked. After working 30 years in tech hardware, watching companies throw away outdated computers while families went without, Loren felt like PCs for People was the answer to a concern that had been nagging him for years.

Most people stumble into charity work or have some dramatic conversion moment. Not Loren. He'd been planning this transition for years.

"I went to a job coach years earlier," he says. "I told him, 'I want to keep working but do something with social impact.' He said, 'You can't just say nonprofit. You've got to pick something.'"

Loren almost chose food banks or housing. Then he stopped himself. "I know nothing about how that works. But I have 30 years in technology. Could I learn about food banks? Sure. But I'd be starting from zero."

His most significant impact would come from what he already knew, not what he wished he knew.

The Economic Threat Everyone Ignored

While politicians talked about the digital divide as if it were someone else's problem, Loren saw what they missed. Loren knew it wasn't about being nice to poor people. The challenge was about economic survival.

"People don't think about what happens next," he says. "A couple of generations ago, you could work at the factory, and make a good living with limited education. Those jobs are disappearing. People without tech skills will just sink deeper and deeper. And that affects all of us."

Picture your neighborhood in ten years. Half the kids can't fill the jobs that exist because they never learned to use computers. What happens to your property values? Your local economy? Your kids' job prospects?

Loren saw this coming. And he found a solution that addresses three problems simultaneously.

PCs for People collects old computers from big companies, schools, and government offices. Instead of letting them rot in landfills, they fix them up and give them to families who can't afford new ones.

Last year alone, 57,000 refurbished computers went to families. That's about 140,000 people who can now work from home, do schoolwork, and apply for jobs. Plus, they kept 6 million pounds of electronics out of dumps.

But here's what makes them different: they don't just hand you a computer and walk away.

"When we give someone a computer, that's when our relationship starts," Loren explains. "People call us and say, 'My mouse doesn't work.' We fix it. Next call: 'Someone told me I need an email account. How do I do that?' Our tech support walks them through setting up Gmail."

They also offer internet for $15 a month and basic computer classes. Loren figured out what most charities miss: a tool without training is just expensive trash.

Building Trust That Pays

Getting old computers isn't the hard part. Every company has closets full of them. The hard part? Building trust with corporations that fear data breaches.

"Every corporation has some way to get rid of old equipment," Loren says. "Some throw it away, some pay recyclers, some sell it online. PCs for People provides them with comprehensive recycling services, along with data destruction so their information stays safe."

The secret isn't just offering secure disposal. In order to achieve the buy in and provide the resources to make the program successful, the person who makes this decision needs to understand that an old refurbished laptop could change people's lives.

"They need to see that what we're doing has value and can still give their company what it needs," Loren says.

At 60-something, leaving a comfortable tech career for a nonprofit made Loren's friends skeptical about his future. His financial advisor wasn't thrilled about the pay cut either.

"The paychecks were bigger at other jobs," he admits. "But I wake up excited to go to work now. It's not just about the paycheck and health insurance. The job satisfaction is indescribable."

Still, there were nights he wondered if he'd made a terrible mistake. What if the nonprofit folded? What if he couldn't adapt? What if he was too old to start over?

The fear was real. But so was Loren's fear of regret.

The Business of Doing Good

Here's what Loren realized: nonprofits are still businesses. They still pay rent, put gas in trucks, and make payroll for 160 employees.

"Passion for the mission is great," he says. "But if you can bring something you already know, that's huge. We still need to balance the books."

His advice to others who are ready for a transition cuts through the fantasy: "Start with 'I want to help people.' Great. But then ask: What specific organization? How can I be a good employee? How does my skill set make a difference? Good intentions don't pay the electric bill. Skills do."

You don't have to quit your job to make a difference. Loren discovered this years before joining PCs for People.

"If you're in purchasing, find suppliers with good hiring practices or sustainable values," he suggests. "You still do your job, still manage the company's money. But now you're also making a difference."

Your Expertise Is Someone's Solution

Loren didn't retrain as a social worker or learn about food distribution. He took 30 years of tech experience and aimed it at a problem that mattered to him.

The result? Families get computers, companies get responsible recycling, the environment gets less waste, and Loren wakes up excited about work.

Most people think making a difference means starting over. Loren proved it means knowing where you fit.

What does it take to connect your expertise with a problem that matters to you and needs solving? Not because it's impossible to solve, but because the people with the skills don't have connections to the people with the needs.

An important place to look is not-for-profit organizations. For example, what about your 10 years in accounting? There are plenty of nonprofits drowning in QuickBooks right now. Your marketing background? A charity has a world-changing program that nobody knows about. Your project management skills? A food bank needs someone who can coordinate 50 volunteers without chaos.

Discovering the bridge between what you know and who needs it can be challenging. However, when you begin thinking about making a change in the focus of your work you're already seeking a bridge. Locating that bridge involves looking inward at your skills and outward at your values. When you identify the skills you want to utilize, it's also important to identify a problem that matters to you. As you move from thinking about doing something new to identifying meaningful work, you are locating your bridge. As you further define your goals, you're getting ready to cross it.

Loren took 30 years of tech expertise and aimed it at a problem that mattered to him: families without computers. He didn't need to retrain or start over. He just needed to connect what he knew with who needed it. Becoming aware of the bridge is the first step—crossing it is your ultimate goal.

In Chapter 7, Jeannie Walters also found a disconnect as she worked with corporate clients. Companies obsess over customer satisfaction scores while their leaders haven't talked to an actual customer in months, some-times years. They make million-dollar decisions about people they've never met, relying on numbers that hide the real story. Her solution? Stop measuring people and start talking to them.

Part Three
People First, Profits Follow

What if the most profitable strategy is to stop trying to be profitable?

Jeannie Walters asked Fortune 100 executives a question that stopped them cold: "When did you last talk to a customer?" Nine out of ten couldn't remember. While companies obsess over satisfaction scores, their leaders make decisions about people they've never met. Jeannie found the "third choice" that lets businesses follow legal rules and treat customers like humans.

Melissa Wilson flipped networking upside down by asking "Why not?" instead of "What's in it for me?" Her approach creates big opportunities by building real relationships based on curiosity and collaboration rather than focusing on what people can do for her.

Billy Dexter spent decades perfecting the art of giving before getting. His formula separates genuine relationship-builders from people who just want access to his network. After 30 years connecting everyone from United Airlines to MTV, Billy knows the difference between people who follow through and those who want shortcuts.

Larry Kaufman discovered something that changed everything about his approach to business: in a company of thousands, he became indispensable by making everyone else successful. While colleagues guarded their secrets and fought for promotions, Larry shared his knowledge freely—and became the person everyone calls when they need help.

You'll see how each pioneer proved that when you put people first, profits actually follow faster than when you chase money directly.

Chapter 7
"When Did You Last Talk to a Customer?"

Companies obsess over customer satisfaction scores, but Jeannie Walters, CEO of Experience Investigators, stuns executives when she asks a different question: "When was the last time you talked to a customer?" Most can't remember.

"Think about how org charts work," Jeannie explains. "The higher up you go, the further away you get from customers."

Walters points out that businesses invest millions in surveys and analytics, yet their leaders haven't had a genuine conversation with a customer in months, sometimes years. "Companies make decisions about people they've never met, relying on numbers that hide the real story."

The Third Choice That Changes Everything

Jeannie's business direction shifted when she asked a Fortune 100 insurance company a simple question: "What's the customer's third choice?"

Marketing and legal departments argued for weeks. Marketing wanted friendly language. Legal demanded formal terms like "the insured." Everyone assumed they had to pick a side.

"We're talking directly to customers now," Jeannie told the chief counsel. "We have online quoting, which we've never done before. So instead of 'the insured,' let's just say 'you.'"

She showed them they didn't have to choose between legal protection and human connection. They could have both. This "Third Choice" thinking became the foundation of Walters' work. Choosing the middle leads to a more acceptable outcome than believing there are only two options.

Jeannie identified another problem the insurance industry calls the "number narrator trap" that was hiding in plain sight.

"A lot of customer experience leaders get painted into a corner where all they do is report on numbers, and they're held accountable for those numbers. But they don't take action to influence those numbers."

She draws a painfully accurate analogy: "It's like telling the carpenter who's ruler is wrong, that it's his fault."

Most organizations confuse measurements with outcomes. "People say, 'We have to get our net promoter score up,' but those are not measurements. Those are outcomes."

The real outcomes? Customers feel heard. The company solves its problems easily. They want to come back.

"I think a lot of times clients focus on the wrong problem." They try to move numbers instead of improving lives.

Creating Fewer Ruined Days

Experience Investigators operates with a mission that sounds almost naive: "to create fewer ruined days for customers."

"When we force customers to call and wait on hold and do all the things we all hate, we chip away at their happiness, and they bring that negativity out into the world. It creates a snowball effect," she explains.

Jeannie pointed out another option: expect your company to make things easy for customers, and they carry that positive energy forward. "If we can help people achieve a goal or feel a certain way, that's what they'll bring out to the world. And then we make the workplace better."

Happy customers create ripple effects. Frustrated customers do too, but in the opposite direction.

Jeannie frequently works across departments. This willingness to ignore boundaries became her most significant advantage.

"Getting out of my lane, looking around and saying, 'Well, maybe if I sit next to the guy who's doing the error messages, I could have an impact on that.'"

Even basic error message wording, which traditionally "made sense to the programmer," became an opportunity to improve the customer experience. This cross-functional thinking was radical in an era when organizations explicitly told people to "stay in their lane."

Jeannie cautions clients against overanalyzing problems and advocates for what she calls a "bias toward action."

"During meetings with my clients and my team, I say, we have a bias toward action. Let's stop talking about it and take action. Sometimes that means taking a small step instead of a big leap. That's still action. That's still progress."

When people say, "That's the way we've always done it," Jeannie challenges them: "That's an excuse. That's not a reason."

Designing Delight, Not Just Fixing Problems

Jeannie doesn't just fix what's broken. She designs experiences that surprise people.

"Disney World still has long lines, but the experience is very different from 20 years ago because of express passes that simplify waiting."

Local examples work too: "When you wait in line at Lou Mitchell's in Chicago on a cold day, the team hands out donut holes so people feel welcome and get a little moment of delight while standing in line."

Customer experience means "being proactive and intentional about the experience you want to deliver."

Our conversation turned to the use of AI in the customer experience world.

While everyone rushes to implement AI, Jeannie sees its real value differently. AI excels at pattern recognition, not replacement.

"If you understand your customer behavior data along with feedback data, you'll better grasp new actions and outcomes."

The psychological insight exposes a common flaw: "We, as humans, will say one thing and behave differently. Using AI to identify those patterns quickly helps us understand and deliver the customer experience people want, even if they don't know how to articulate it."

Still, Jeannie stays realistic about AI's limits. "Humans are very nuanced, which means many layers go into how we make decisions that I don't think connect with AI yet."

The Revolution Nobody Sees Coming

Jeannie points out something others miss: Customer experience is evolving from a department to a company-wide skill.

"You can't just have a customer experience team anymore," she predicts. "When competition gets fierce, and it's intensifying, every department needs to think about the customer: Marketing, Legal, IT, operations. Everyone."

Companies that figure this out first will dominate. Those that keep customer experience locked in a department will disappear.

"Five years from now, having a separate customer experience department will be like having a separate quality department. It will be everyone's responsibility, or it won't work at all."

Walters witnessed this shift towards customer experience as part of the corporate culture firsthand through an experience with an employee from a younger generation. "I have a powerful memory of a younger person who worked for us, and she came in a little disheveled and said, 'Oh, I stayed at my boyfriend's and didn't bring all my stuff,' and I thought to myself, 'Wow! I would have never said that.'"

This openness represents a broader transformation taking place in the workplace: "People are more comfortable acknowledging that we're whole people." The shift from compartmentalized professional personas to integrated honesty marks one of the most significant changes in modern workplace culture.

Your Customer Blind Spot

Right now, you're making decisions about people you've never met. You study their data, analyze their behavior, and measure their satisfaction. Knowing and measuring only gets you so far, which can leave a company vulnerable. The most critical question you want to ask in the future is, When did I last have an actual conversation with them?"

The next time you feel stuck between two bad options, such as formal language or friendly tone, efficiency or empathy, cost-cutting or customer service, stop. Ask yourself: "What's the third choice?"

Jeannie found it in a single word: "you" instead of "the insured." Three letters that kept lawyers happy and made customers feel human.

Do you wonder where you'll find the third choice? It's not in reports or surveys. You'll find it in conversations with real people who use what you create.

Pick up the phone. Schedule a coffee. Listen to someone outside your building, not on your org chart, and spend less time focused on your Key Performance Indicators.

The gap between what customers say in surveys and what they tell you face-to-face will shock you. That gap is where you'll find your next opportunity.

Jeannie proved that when you stop measuring people and start talking to them, everything changes and your blind spots disappear. Your real opportunities emerge. Your customers become partners instead of numbers.

Melissa G. Wilson noticed the same blind spots in book creation. Authors wrote alone, promoted alone, succeeded or failed alone. Nobody questioned why it had to be that way. So Melissa built something different —a system where every book becomes a bridge, every author becomes a connector, and success becomes contagious. The nine-year-old girl who kept asking "Why doesn't somebody do that?" finally grew up and did it herself.

.

Chapter 8
"Why Not?"

Melissa was nine years old when she first realized she saw the world differently. While other children played with toys, she scribbled down whimsical ideas, asked questions that made adults uncomfortable, and wondered why nobody seemed to notice the gaps. These missing pieces could make everything better.

"Why doesn't somebody do that?" became her constant refrain. "Why doesn't this community have these offerings?" She wasn't trying to be difficult; she was genuinely curious about a world that seemed full of untapped possibilities.

Looking at her now, after decades as a publisher, author, and what she's come to call a "connector," it's clear that this early curiosity wasn't just childhood precocity. It became the foundation of everything she would build. But the path to understanding that gift wasn't always easy.

Learning to Ask Why

Growing up in a household where questions weren't always welcome taught Melissa that sometimes you have to find your answers. Her parents weren't necessarily happy all the time, and as one of four children, she quickly learned that her constant "Whys" could be met with frustration rather than encouragement. But she couldn't stop asking. The curiosity was too intense.

Melissa was always looking for ways to make things better in her household environment, standing between her sisters when tensions rose, trying to smooth the rough edges of family life. Her younger sister and brother are still with her today, and they're incredibly close. They've worked through whatever happened in their youth because they're amazing people, and she's grateful they're in her life.

But those early experiences taught Melissa something crucial: when you can't change your circumstances, you can change how you respond to them. You can choose to see opportunities instead of obstacles.

Networking Values Foundation

This perspective shaped the core values that would guide everything Melissa did: curiosity, collaboration, creativity, and integrity. Integrity meant doing what you say you're going to do-and then actually doing it. It meant staying true to your values even when the world gets weird, sometimes going left when everybody else is going right.

She remembers walking down a hill once with her family among about fifty people following a guide. Paper trash was scattered all along the path. People had thrown things on the ground instead of putting them in garbage cans. Melissa picked up every single piece while everyone else walked past. Looking around at the indifferent faces, she thought, "This is the difference between me and everyone else." It wasn't conceit; it was recognition of a fundamental difference in how she saw responsibility and possibility.

Finding Her Professional Path

That difference in perspective shaped Melissa's entire career trajectory. She started with an undergraduate degree in social work, sociology, and English, then pursued a master's in English. But she was always looking for gaps. These are places where she could contribute something that somebody hadn't already noticed.

She discovered she was early to technical writing when computers were just becoming widespread. Suddenly, Melissa was rewriting user manuals for companies like Babcock and Wilcox, transforming incomprehensible technical jargon into something people could use. The dean at the University of Akron noticed her skill and recommended her to BF Goodrich, where, instead of earning $38,000 annually, she could make $50,000 working just one day a week, redoing their computer manuals.

She kept asking, "Why not?" Why not teach writing at the college level? Why not get a law degree? Why not start her own business? Each question led to another opportunity, another way to contribute.

But life also threw her curveballs. Her spouse suffered from nervous breakdowns, creating enormous stress as she tried everything to help while also caring for her two sons. Eventually, Melissa had to make the difficult decision to move on, recognizing that she couldn't save someone who wasn't ready to be saved, and she had responsibilities to her children.

Riding the Wave of Change

Sometimes the hardest periods of our lives coincide with the most significant opportunities. As Melissa was navigating personal challenges and building a business, she found herself at the forefront of an incredible shift. When she started, women owned only 17% of all small businesses. By around 2000, that number had jumped to almost 50%. She rode the wave of change in Chicago, working with the state of Illinois to help other entrepreneurs and teach entrepreneurship.

It was during this time that Melissa developed Networlding, where she helped many large companies, such as AT&T, Heidrick, Motorola, CDW, Office Depot, Fifth-Third Bank, and many more, build the Networlding path of "Creating mutually beneficial relationships to create transformational opportunities." Here, others learned to create life-long vibrant networks instead of business card or small talk exchanges. Through Networlding bootcamps and coaching, Melissa helped company leaders build collaborative networks that could transform not just businesses, but communities and lives.

The Power of Connection

Melissa's first major publishing success came with Dearborn Publishing, which later became Kaplan. Those early books opened doors she never could have imagined. She also found herself presenting at LinkedIn when they had only 80 people, a Dorothy-like experience that showed her what it meant to be at the front door of opportunity.

She also worked with leaders at Twitter in its early days. Melissa built a variety of Networlding training sessions, eventually licensed by Yale University's Graduate School of Business. But what excited Melissa most wasn't the prestige or recognition. It was the realization that she could share the Networlding process with individuals at various stages of their careers, from those just starting to fast-growth entrepreneurs and senior leaders in Fortune 500 companies, to help them create their Networlds and unlock transformational opportunities.

Her book "Networlding" became more than just a title. It became a philosophy. Melissa spent seven years on the Women's Graduate Advisory Board at the University of Chicago, even though she didn't attend there. They made her one of six outstanding women of the decade and treated her like family. At regular panel discussions, they named Melissa "The Cleanup Batter" because she was last to speak. She would take the opportunity to tie together her other panelists' thoughts, adding them to her own, and help the audience gain a deeper understanding of the subjects.

Talking Authors Off the Ledge

Over the past fifteen years, Melissa transitioned from being an author with ten traditionally published books, six traditional publishers, a New York agent, and one of her books on *Oprah*, to becoming a hybrid publisher for thought leaders. So far, she has helped 170+ leaders, many of whom you would assume would brim with confidence. Melissa discovered these excellent leaders would need the same support and hand-holding as anyone else she worked with in the companies where she provided training. There's something profoundly moving about watching Melissa help someone recognize their voice and trust that their story matters. Every book becomes a tool for opening doors, meeting new people, and exploring new places, exactly what her nine-year-old self was seeking.

Melissa's Unofficial Motto: Where Others See Roadblocks, Melissa Sees Pathways

When faced with obstacles, she automatically starts looking for a way around or over them. "You can't leverage from weakness," she often says. "You have to leverage your strength. Otherwise, it's like trying to build on sticks in the sand instead of a solid foundation."

When setbacks occur, Melissa has learned to feel them fully without brushing them away, but also without beating herself up. She's watched too many people call themselves idiots when things go wrong. Instead, she looks for the balance, for the places of strength that still exist, and builds from there.

The Crisis of Connection

Melissa believes we are and will continue to face what she calls a genuine crisis of connection, isolation, and communication. People are more linked than ever through technology, yet more isolated than ever from meaningful relationships. Melissa wants to address this loneliness, which is why she's so passionate about her latest idea for supporting thought leader book authors called "Book Riffing." This activity brings authors together, primarily online, to read excerpts from their books, creating a vibration and energy that fosters deeper connections among participants.

As Melissa shares with interested audiences, "When you read from a book, even just one page, something magical happens. It's an immersive experience that amplifies social media posts, reels, and other video formats. She envisions events where, instead of traditional book clubs reading one book, participants sample multiple authors, connecting to various content and building community around the shared love of words and ideas.

The Vision Moving Forward

Melissa is currently helping develop a 550-seat theater in Elmhurst, Illinois called Encore Performing Arts Center. It will focus on live performances, often referred to as "Intimate Performances." She believes we're going to see more immersive experiences where place makes a difference. Here, being physically present with people and having facilitators who are passionate about connecting others helps the books come alive. The future, in her view, isn't about competing for attention in an increasingly fragmented digital landscape. It's about creating spaces-physical and metaphorical-where genuine connection can happen. It's about recognizing that we don't have to choose between embracing technology and preserving human connection. We can have both.

The Greatest Good for the Greatest Number

At its core, everything Melissa does stems from a single driving force: the desire to create the greatest good for the greatest number of people. She sees things as opportunities and possibilities and genuinely doesn't understand why others don't see them too. Melissa believes even big problems can be solved with ingenuity, camaraderie, and collaboration.

Her advice to other author-entrepreneurs is simple: if you get real joy from writing, that should be your number one purpose. Visit your local libraries. They don't just accept books from local authors; they buy them. Get involved in your community. Join marketing support groups for authors. Consider immersive experiences and live events.

Most importantly, remember that you don't have to spend a fortune to create a book, so why not do it? Every memoir becomes a healing tool while you write it. Every book becomes a bridge to new relationships and opportunities.

The Butterfly Effect

Melissa has butterfly wallpaper in her home, a reminder of transformation and the beauty that emerges from periods of apparent dormancy. Right now, she believes we're in a cocoon phase for authors and creators. There's so much change happening, so much uncertainty, but also unprecedented opportunity.

Like monarchs emerging from chrysalis, she sees a generation of authors ready to explode into the world with new models of connection, new ways of building community, and new approaches to sharing stories that matter. They're not competing with each other for a limited audience. They're collaborating to expand the very idea of what books and authors can be.

When asked about her legacy, Melissa doesn't point to the individual books she's written or published, though she's proud of those. Instead, she talks about the ball of yarn she created in Chicago, connecting Motorola with Office Depot with American Express and twenty-two chambers of commerce in the north suburbs. She remembers the moment when people realized they had more in common than they thought, when everything changed because of connection.

That's what Melissa wants to leave behind: a world where people celebrate curiosity, where collaboration creates transformation, where the nine-year-old asking "why not?" is encouraged rather than silenced. A world where we build bridges instead of walls, where we see pathways instead of roadblocks, where we create the greatest good for the greatest number.

Because ultimately, that's what pioneers do. They don't just see the world as it is. They see it as it could be, and then they roll up their sleeves and build the bridges to get there. And in Melissa's case, she's spent her entire career not just building those bridges but teaching others how to build them too.Melissa built bridges between authors, communities, and opportunities by refusing to accept that connection had to be transactional. She created spaces where people could share their work and build relationships that mattered.

Advice from Melissa

1. Ask "Why Not?" Instead of "Why Can't I?"

What it means: When others see limitations, ask "Why not try this?" instead of accepting roadblocks. **Why it matters:** This single question shift opened every door in Melissa's career—from technical writing to law school to building her own business. Most people stop at obstacles. Melissa used them as starting points for new possibilities. You can do the same with whatever's blocking you right now.

2. Pick Up the Trash Nobody Else Sees

What it means: Notice problems others ignore and fix them, even when it's not your job. **Why it matters:** Melissa's willingness to clean up literal trash on a hiking trail revealed her secret weapon: she takes responsibility for things others walk past. This mindset led her to spot gaps in technical writing, publishing, and networking that became her biggest opportunities. The problems you're uniquely positioned to solve are hiding in plain sight.

3. Build from Your Strengths, Not Your Weaknesses

What it means: "You can't build on sticks in the sand instead of a solid foundation." **Why it matters:** When setbacks happen, most people focus on what went wrong. Melissa looks for what's still working and builds from there. She doesn't brush away problems, but she doesn't beat herself up either. This approach helped her navigate personal challenges while building a business that helped Fortune 500 companies.

4. Create Connections, Not Transactions

What it means: Focus on bringing people together for mutual benefit, not just personal gain. **Why it matters:** Melissa's "Networlding" approach—creating lasting relationships instead of business card exchanges—got licensed by Yale's Business School and helped her work with everyone from LinkedIn to major corporations. In a world where people feel more isolated despite being more connected, the ability to create genuine human connections becomes your competitive advantage.

The Bottom Line

Melissa proved that curiosity isn't just a nice trait—it's a business strategy. Her nine-year-old question "Why doesn't somebody do that?" became the foundation for a career spent turning problems into opportunities and helping others do the same. The gaps you see that frustrate you? Those are your biggest opportunities waiting to happen.

But what happens when you take that same philosophy of connection and apply it to building multiple powerful networks? Billy Dexter discovered that the secret to building powerful networks wasn't collecting business cards or LinkedIn connections. It was something most professionals get backwards: you network to give, not to get.

Chapter 9
Network to Give: Not to Get

illy Dexter, a master at building networking groups that last, in many cases, decades, can quickly spot the difference between people who want genuine relationships and those who just want access to his network. After 30 years of connecting people across industries from United Airlines to MTV, Deloitte to Monster.com, Billy developed what he calls the "run the route" test.

"It's like the trust between a quarterback and receiver," he explains. "The quarterback throws to a spot, trusting the receiver will get there, vs. some people want to get straight to the opportunities without building a relationship."

Billy learned this lesson the hard way. He once made an introduction to someone with whom he had a 20-year friendship without his usual vetting. His longtime friend not only misused Billy's contact but also damaged the business relationships Billy had built.

"My contact came back to me and said, 'So this is your guy. Let me tell you what your guy did.'" The incident cost Billy a client relationship for several years.

To better understand what led to Billy learning this lesson later in his career let's take a step back and look at how his career began.

Billy's Early Career: The Winter That Changed Everything

Billy's journey to master network builder began during a winter break when he stayed alone on Michigan State's campus while everyone else went home for the holidays. It wasn't about having nowhere to go. It was about choosing his future over his comfort.

With barely enough money for a ride back to Detroit and uncertain about getting back for spring semester, Billy made a choice that would define his approach to life. He told everyone he was going home for Christmas, then quietly stayed behind in an empty dormitory, working at J.C. Penney and studying alone while snow fell outside his window.

"During these quieter moments, I adopted the philosophy that you network to give, not to get," Billy reflects. "I knew I had to do whatever it takes, which meant staying on campus during winter break, building relationships, and earning money."

His mother was disappointed, but Billy knew something others didn't: relationships and opportunities don't wait for convenient timing.

The Crossroads Revelation

Billy's breakthrough came while working as the youngest assistant director in the largest career services office in the country at Michigan State. He was living his dream, helping students prepare for interviews and navigate their futures.

"I was 120% into that," he recalls. "The best job I ever had."

But one evening, working late as usual, Billy walked through the offices of his colleagues. He noticed they all had PhDs with 15-25 years of tenure.

"It hit me that this could be my future life. Pursuing degrees and dedicating time to this institution is where I will be for the rest of my career. And it scared the hell out of me because I knew I loved this place, I loved this job, but something inside of me said, 'Bill, there's more for you.'"

The realization wasn't about dissatisfaction. It was about recognizing a fundamental truth: growth requires discomfort, and comfort can become a cage.

Seeing What Others Missed

Across multiple industries, Billy discovered something that would become his signature: he could see talent that others missed. This was partly because he had a keen sense of awareness of talents among diverse groups of people.

"Early on, I recognized how organizations needed to embrace diversity. I saw that way before other people." When organizations claimed they "can't find folks" or that diverse talent doesn't exist, Billy's response was simple: "I am one of those people. I see these folks all around. They're my friends. What? Are you kidding?"

Billy built diverse networks since his college days, not as a diversity initiative but as a natural result of his authentic relationship-building approach. Over the course of his career, Billy eventually created a model that brought his approach to life and easy for others to learn.

The Win-Win-Win Philosophy

Billy's most transformative contribution is his "Win-Win-Win" approach. When people ask Billy to refer someone in his network, he asks himself three questions:

1. What's the win for the person I'm connecting with?
2. What's the win for the organization?
3. What's the potential win for me?

"My win may be years down the road or may be immediate. But I ask myself those questions before making each connection."

The Circle of Friends Pioneer

Billy's ability to spot gaps in networks and create solutions shows up in his creation of the Circle of Friends golf group, now in its 25th year. Recognizing that he had little in common with fellow members at his country club beyond golf and that his friends couldn't afford club memberships, Billy created an alternative.

"I went to two other guys, and we started a group. The connection was golf, but the second win was the network we were going to create."

Twenty-five years later, the group continues to grow. "You've got guys that are doing business together, traveling together, and hiring each other. And the third win is that we'll be friends for life."

Oftentimes, people approach Billy intending to request connections from his valuable network. In these cases, Billy often conducts his personal "Authenticity Test" to determine whether or not someone will, as they say in football, "run the route." His criteria for authentic connections include finding common ground and showing authenticity.

"When I meet with people asking for connections, I listen for specific information. Are they willing to speak openly about who they are? Do they communicate their future goals? Do they demonstrate vulnerability and share what they struggle with?"

Assuming the answers to these questions are yes, Billy still tends to be skeptical. Billy runs "The Integrity Test" to better understand the connection's core values. When we began our conversation about core values, Billy shared his immediately. "Integrity is the number one value that supersedes everything for me. Don't make it about you, be authentic, don't take shortcuts, always try to do the right thing."

People test Billy's integrity repeatedly. He shares the story of a friend who approached him with a fraudulent invoicing scheme, asking Billy to have his firm pay fake invoices in exchange for kickbacks.

"It was a non-starter, but what upset me most was that my 'friend' would even think that I would be the type of guy who would do that."

That incident taught Billy something important about the people he'd surrounded himself with. It took a global pandemic to teach him something even more critical about himself.

When COVID-19 sent everyone home, Billy discovered he could be more productive working remotely. He could focus without interruptions, handle more calls, and check off more tasks. But something felt wrong.

"For the time during COVID, I felt like I was only at 60 to 70% energy. I realized that I need to be around people. I get my energy that way. That's how I thrive."

The pandemic forced Billy to understand what truly fueled his approach to business. It was about human connection, which led him to write out a simple formula: Connections + Relationships = Opportunity. But he's careful to distinguish between the two.

"A relationship begins with a commitment between connections at some level that we're going to stay connected, or we're going to do some things together, or I'm going to share referrals."

Mistakes that Kill Your Network?

Waiting Until You Need Something: Billy's most significant insight is that "Networking is not something you do on Thursday from five to seven. Practice this every day." Don't wait until you're out of a job to start building connections."

Skipping the "Run the Route" Test: Like the trust between a quarterback and receiver, strong professional relationships require mutual reliability. Don't waste time on people who are "looking through you" to get to opportunities.

Forgetting Win-Win-Win: Before making any introduction, ask: What's the win for person A? What's the win for person B? What's the potential win for me? Skipping this step risks damaging your reputation due to poor connections.

Step One: Flip the Script

Billy's formula evolved into much more than one or two networks. To date, Billy has formed 21 Networking Hubs that range from golf to theatre to business to travel, including activities like smoking cigars and more.

What does networking look like when you "Flip the Script?" It begins with asking yourself different questions, such as, "How can I help this person?" Focus on giving first, and the getting takes care of itself.

Billy built his career by giving before getting, and creating networks that lasted decades. But what happens when you take that same generous spirit and apply it to an industry known for being cutthroat and transactional? In Chapter 9, Larry Kaufman discovered that even in the world of mergers and acquisitions, treating people like humans instead of deal-makers could transform an entire business model.

Chapter 10
How to Become Indispensable

Larry Kaufman sat in his office at 8 PM, staring at spreadsheets while the building emptied around him. After 15 years away from Jefferson Wells, he returned to the same company in 2017. He had a bigger title, better pay, but something gnawed at him.

In a 20-billion-dollar corporation with thousands of employees, he felt invisible.

"I could be a little dot," Larry admits. "I could easily get lost in a vast pool of employees worldwide. But I'm not."

If he disappeared tomorrow, would anyone notice?

The Fear That Became Larry's Breakthrough

Larry's biggest fear wasn't failure, though he did fear he'd go unnoticed. He'd watched colleagues fight for promotions, guard their secrets, and make themselves the only person who could solve specific problems. They'd climb the ladder, then get fired in the subsequent layoffs.

"If you lead with yourself, you will leave with yourself," Larry realized.

So he tried something different. Instead of climbing the ladder himself, he started helping everyone else climb theirs.

Larry's first test came with the toughest group: analytical CPAs who needed to become salespeople.

"My claim to fame was converting CPAs into true salespeople. Difficult because they're very analytical, very matter-of-fact: 'This is the way it is.'"

Sales training failed with this group. Larry knew he had to offer something more interesting.

Instead of forcing them into a sales mold, he tried something that felt risky: "We exchanged information about our respective knowledge areas. I shared what I knew about sales, and they shared what they knew about being an accountant. I got to learn from them, and they got to learn from me."

His stomach churned during those first training sessions. What if they didn't buy in? What if his problem-solving approach looked weak compared to pushy sales tactics?

Something magical happened. The CPAs started connecting with clients by solving problems instead of pushing products. Sales went up. More importantly, they started coming to Larry for advice on everything, including personal and work issues.

"I came back seven years ago, and many of the people I've trained work with and for me today and still use methodologies I created in 1998."

The Solutions That Changed Everything

In 2017, Larry watched potential clients walk away because they couldn't afford the company's $10,000 up-front fee. He saw a gap but worried about proposing something that might look like discounting.

"What if we let them access our expertise for just an hour at a time?" he suggested in a meeting. His colleagues looked skeptical.

Larry created "Knowledge Exchange Services,"

designed to allow clients to tap into expertise without huge commitments.

"It's a door opener and a way to get to know each other without a big up-front payment," Larry explains.

Here's how it works: "We'd go to that meeting, and, after listening for awhile would ask,

'Well, did you do this, that and the other?'

'No.'

'Oh, that's going to be a problem.'

'Can you help us?' And all of a sudden, we have three people helping them."

Larry feared this would hurt bigger contracts. Instead, clients who started with one-hour consultations became his biggest accounts.

During COVID-19, Larry observed leaders issuing generic "reach out anytime" messages that were taken seriously by no one. He decided to take them seriously himself.

When a new leader joined the company, Larry sent a message: "I'd love to spend half an hour getting to know you and see how I could be helpful in your new role."

Most ignored him. But some responded. And those conversations changed everything.

"Whatever issues you're experiencing, challenges in life, or you need me to chat with your daughter about their career, or help them get an internship, let me help," became Larry's standard offer to his team.

His colleagues thought he was crazy. "You're not a counselor," one told him. "You're supposed to be managing sales numbers."

The results spoke louder than skepticism. Larry's team turnover dropped. Their sales improved. More importantly, people throughout the massive organization started calling him "LinkedIn Larry" and "the go-to guy."

Senior leadership began reaching out for help on personal matters. In a company of thousands, Larry had become the go-to person because he shared his knowledge about everything, not just work.

Larry's Lesson Learned About Creating Value

"Have you noticed there's more kindness out there?" Larry asks. "People are more caring. There are even people working remotely who value your willingness to connect: Ask them, 'How are you doing? I know it's tough to be sitting alone at your computer all day."

Larry's prediction: "The leaders who win are the ones

who have that empathy and think that way about their teams."

Early in his career, Larry almost lost a major client because he tried to be the most intelligent person in the room. He pitched a complex solution that showcased his expertise but overlooked the client's actual needs.

"I was so focused on proving my value that I forgot to create value," he reflects.

The client walked away. Larry's boss wasn't happy. That's when Larry learned the difference between being impressive and being helpful.

"I can't do it alone. I need that sphere of influence around me that could do all those things that I can't do."

That failure became Larry's foundation. It taught him that the most powerful question in business isn't "How can I prove my worth?" but "How can I help you succeed?"

Everything Larry built after that moment focused on developing new strategies to make selling easy for CPA's. First, he taught CPA's how to lead conversations about Knowledge Exchange Services, and his concierge approach to leadership. These new ideas resulted from understanding that becoming indispensable isn't about what you can do. It's about who you can help succeed.

Larry proved that becoming the person everyone calls starts with a genuine interest in others' success and the guts to lead with service instead of self-promotion.

Looking Forward

Start where you are. Look for problems others aren't solving. Remove barriers that prevent people from accessing your expertise. Larry frequently invites people he meets to ask who might be a good connection for an introduction and then follows up immediately.

Ask yourself: If I disappeared tomorrow, would anyone notice? If the answer scares you, start helping someone else succeed today.

Larry built influence by making everyone around him more successful, and even turned analytical CPAs into relationship-builders that became rainmakers. But what happens when you take that same others-first approach and apply it to an industry built on spreadsheets, speed, and beating your competitors?

Natalie Shmulik discovered that in a high-stakes world of running an entrepreneurship incubator. She learned, the secret to winning isn't building something better, it's nurturing your entrepreneurs as whole people vs. only business people.

Part Four
Building Things That Outlast You

What if the worst mistake successful people make is thinking small?

So far, you've seen pioneers change their careers and companies. These next three pioneers figured out something bigger: how to create things that keep helping people long after they're gone.

In chapter 11, you'll learn about the moment Natalie Shmulik was falling apart on her restaurant's kitchen floor at 2 AM and became painfully aware of something that would save thousands of entrepreneurs from the same breakdown.

Shawn Campbell got tired of colleagues calling her radio stations "cute little projects." Those comments sparked her to create 700 community stations nationwide.

And our final pioneer? She looked at an entire industry built on competition and outdated laws and asked a dangerous question: "What if we did the exact opposite?"

You'll see how they moved beyond personal success to build things that multiply their impact forever.

Chapter 11
The Entrepreneur Whisperer

The Problem Everyone Refused to See

"Nobody can prepare you for what you go through internally as an entrepreneur."

—Natalie Shmulik, Former CEO of The Hatchery Chicago

While everyone else built business incubators focused on technical skills, financial planning, and market analysis, Natalie Shmulik saw the real problem: entrepreneurs were breaking down mentally before their businesses ever had a chance to fail.

She knew from her experience as a restaurant owner, that the biggest threat to entrepreneurial success isn't lack of business knowledge. It's the psychological warfare that happens inside every founder's head.

"You can give entrepreneurs all the technical tools they need. Any incubator will provide licensing, certification, and insurance. What very few prepare you for is the loneliness, the self-doubt, the leadership skills that you don't realize you need."

Natalie designed The Hatchery Chicago, an incubator focused on food and beverage, around a simple principle: treat the human first, the business second.

Her realization hit at 2 AM on a Tuesday, sitting on her restaurant's kitchen floor after another 16-hour day. The books are balanced. She had trained her staff. The food was excellent. But Natalie was falling apart, and no business school had prepared her for that part.

"I could be prepared financially and legally. I could have taken all the necessary steps. However, nobody can prepare you for what you go through internally as an entrepreneur to try to survive business ownership."

That night on the kitchen floor, Natalie made herself a promise: if she ever had the chance to help other entrepreneurs, she'd address the part everyone else ignored. Natalie prioritized assisting entrepreneurs with the psychological breakdown that happens when you're responsible for everything and everyone.

Natalie's Shocking Discovery About Incubators

Years later, when she started investigating business incubators, the proof was everywhere. "A lot of individuals run incubation programs who have no experience with entrepreneurship," she observed. "There's a plethora of consultants. There aren't as many people who have been there and done it."

She watched entrepreneurs come to programs "in tears, confide in us, sometimes see our support as therapeutic." They didn't need another business plan template. What they needed was someone who understood that starting a business can be just as mentally challenging as it is financially.

Natalie didn't stop with psychological support. Every decision she made for The Hatchery went against what everyone else believed worked. When creating The Hatchery, Natalie rejected wealthy neighborhoods with established foot traffic. Instead, she picked East Garfield Park on Chicago's West Side-a choice that made other business advisors cringe.

"A lot of groups would never think to invest in a neighborhood where they knew it would be an uphill battle," Natalie explains. "We flipped that on its head and said, we're going to build in a community that could best benefit from these resources."

The Hatchery itself reflects Natalie's unconventional thinking. Walking into the 67,000-square-foot space, you're hit first by the rich aroma of roasting coffee, baking bread, and simmering sauces. Nothing that resembled the sterile scent of corporate offices. The main floor buzzes with the sounds of industrial mixers, the hiss of espresso machines, and entrepreneurs calling across workstations to share taste tests.

The Hatchery feels like a combination of working kitchen, laboratory, and neighborhood community center rather than the typical startup atmosphere of ping pong tables and motivational posters. Entrepreneurs work side by side in shared commercial kitchen space, and they gather in comfortable seating areas that look more like a friend's living room than a conference room.

The logic was simple: "There are plenty of resources downtown. But in East Garfield Park, there are none."

She also redefined success. While other incubators measured success by business launches and revenue, Natalie redefined it entirely.

"We talk about success as launching a successful business. However, we also describe success as completing the program and ultimately concluding that this is not the business for you. It's a satisfying feeling to know you tried it."

Natalie's mission for The Hatchery was not to promote a feel-good philosophy. She also wanted to help entrepreneurs make informed decisions when they realize their dream is a doomed venture, and save them from losing their life savings.

Suppose Natalie made an incorrect bet by focusing on the psychological issues, the location choice, and redefining success metrics. Would the Hatchery have succeeded? Not. Nor would other cities start copying her approach.

The Hot Sauce Revelation and Other Sideways Solutions

Before mental health in the workplace became trendy in business, Natalie built emotional support into her incubator. Entrepreneurs acquire technical skills, but they also receive help coping with the isolation and self-doubt that kills more businesses than bad financial planning.

Her community-first location choice proved equally bright. By choosing East Garfield Park, she built an incubator that serves the community instead of extracting from it. Word-of-mouth marketing that money can't buy flows from loyalty created by genuine service. Entrepreneurs who succeed become ambassadors for both the program and the neighborhood.

Natalie's own "weird" thinking became a template for helping entrepreneurs embrace their unconventional approaches. "I would have to find roundabout ways to come up with a solution. But in certain circumstances, that worked in my favor, because then I was able to see a completely different perspective."

Here's how it works in practice: When a hot sauce entrepreneur came to Natalie struggling with distribution, traditional business advice would have focused on logistics, pricing, or marketing channels. Natalie asked an unexpected question: "What if your distribution problem is a story problem?"

She helped the entrepreneur realize that customers didn't just want hot sauce. They also wanted to feel connected to the maker's grandmother's recipe and family heritage. "I told him, 'Your grandmother's story is your competitive advantage. People can buy hot sauce anywhere, but they can't buy your family's story anywhere else,'" Natalie recalls. The entrepreneur started including family photos and recipe cards with each bottle. Sales tripled, not because they reached more stores, but because customers became emotionally invested in the product.

Looking at problems sideways rather than head-on comes from Natalie's struggles with traditional learning. "In school, I always had to take the long way to the answer, but sometimes that long way revealed things the direct path missed."

"I used to think there was something wrong with me because I couldn't learn the way everyone else did," she admits. "Teachers would show us the 'right' way to solve problems, and my brain just wouldn't work that way. I'd get to the same answer, but I'd take these weird detours that confused everyone."

She teaches entrepreneurs to use their unique problem-solving styles instead of forcing them into standard business approaches. "Now I tell entrepreneurs, 'Your weird way of thinking isn't a bug, it's a feature. That's probably your biggest advantage.'"

Natalie's systems thinking also paid off in another area where she excelled: recognizing that policy changes, rather than product innovations, are the most significant drivers of disruption in the food and beverage sector. "Everyone always asks, 'What's the most disruptive thing in the industry?' And I think people forget that it's not necessarily an idea. It's policy."

"I'm the person reading policy documents at night instead of watching Netflix," she laughs. "My husband thinks I'm crazy, but that's where the real opportunities hide. While other incubators were chasing the next trendy superfood in 2018, I was preparing my entrepreneurs for cottage food law changes."

When the Illinois Cottage Food Operation Act expanded in 2019, allowing home-based food businesses to sell directly to consumers, Natalie's entrepreneurs were ready. "I saw the policy discussions happening at the state level and knew this was going to change everything for small food producers," she explains. They had already established customer bases and grasped the regulatory requirements, while their competitors scrambled to catch up.

Understanding policy changes shaped her career advice. She advises young professionals to create opportunities through direct action rather than waiting for ideal job postings.

"Every role I've had, I've had to create it. The job market is very restrictive because it uses information about what already exists. It's not going to introduce you to what doesn't exist yet, because you might be the person who creates it."

Her advice comes from personal experience. When Natalie first wanted to work in food and entrepreneurship, that job category didn't exist. "I remember calling my mom after college, crying because I couldn't figure out what I was supposed to do with my life. I knew I loved food and helping people build businesses, but there was no job posting for 'food entrepreneur supporter.'"

"So I just started doing it anyway," she says. "First through my restaurant, then by meeting other food entrepreneurs at farmers' markets and coffee shops. I kept asking them what kind of support they wished they had. Eventually, I realized that designing The Hatchery in my head was the support system I wished I'd had, but didn't exist anywhere, so I had to build it."

Natalie proved that the most successful pioneers solve human problems that show up in business contexts. She saw what everyone else missed: entrepreneurs aren't just business operators, they're humans under extreme psychological pressure.

By treating the whole person, she creates success rates that traditional approaches can't match. More importantly, she's built a model that other cities and industries now copy.

What Natalie's Story Teaches Us

Your "Weird" is Your Weapon: Natalie's learning differences became her greatest strength. The round-about thinking that frustrated her teachers in third grade became the exact skill she needed to help entrepreneurs solve problems sideways. What you see as your biggest flaw might be your competitive advantage.

Fix the Root, Not the Symptoms: While everyone else focused on the business skills gap, Natalie addressed the underlying psychological breakdown. Most people solve surface problems; pioneers dig deeper to find what's broken. The entrepreneurs coming to programs in tears didn't need better business plans. The missing piece was invisible. Food entrepreneurs need help from someone who understands that starting a business can impact their mental health.

Serve First, Scale Later: Natalie chose East Garfield Park not because it was profitable, but because it needed what she offered. When you serve authentically, loyalty follows. Her focus on community need over profit potential created word-of-mouth marketing that money can't buy.

Redefine Success on Your Terms: "Deciding not to start a business" as success challenges everything the startup world believes. Sometimes the bravest thing you can do is protect someone from a bad decision. Sometimes saving someone's life matters more than celebrating another launch.

Create the Job That Doesn't Exist: Natalie didn't wait for someone to post a job for "food entrepreneur supporter." She followed her curiosity, built the solution she wished existed, and created an entire industry category. Your perfect opportunity doesn't exist yet; however, this is your opportunity to make it.

Stop trying to fix the obvious problems everyone else is fixing. Look for the human element that everyone's ignoring. Ask yourself: What's the psychological or emotional reality that everyone's pretending doesn't exist?

That's where your most promising opportunity lies.

Natalie built The Hatchery by treating entrepreneurs as whole humans, not just business plans. But what happens when you take that same human-centered approach and apply it to an industry that had forgotten why it mattered in the first place? Shawn Campbell watched commercial radio strip away everything that made radio special. The live connection, community engagement, and human curation that helped people discover music they loved. So she did something radical: she brought it all back.

Chapter 12
What Happened to Good Radio?

The Insult That Changed Everything

"Oh, Shawn, I just really admire the fact that you've stuck to it so long at these little radio stations."

The backhanded compliment hit Shawn Campbell hard, yet she knew she was doing the right thing. She didn't care that her fellow radio professionals saw this idea as settling for less. Shawn knew that genuine human connection, community engagement, and musical discovery would be more valuable in the long run.

That moment crystallized a choice Shawn had been wrestling with throughout her career: follow the conventional path toward commercial success, or build something that mattered. The comment stung because it revealed how her colleagues saw her work as a failure instead of pioneering.

Ironically, none of those fellow radio professionals dared take the risks Shawn Campbell took.

When Shawn launched CHIRP Radio in 2007, she wasn't just starting another radio station. She was solving a problem most people had accepted as inevitable: commercial radio stripped away everything that made radio special.

The biggest challenge wasn't technical; it was about changing minds. "Often, people didn't quite get what we were doing. We'd hear comments like, 'Oh, that's just a jukebox. That's just like an iTunes playlist."

Industry professionals often missed what CHIRP was building. "Sometimes the response was condescending, like, 'Oh, that internet radio station?' It took time for people to respect not just me, but what we'd built."

Shawn's big idea was surprising: to innovate in radio, they needed to go back to what worked before everyone forgot why it mattered.

"What we always talk about is that we embrace the traditional values of radio," Shawn says. "In a way, it's breaking the mold. But in a way, what we're doing is just going back to what radio used to be."

"While commercial radio automated everything, CHIRP went live. While others eliminated DJs, CHIRP made them personalities. While the industry chased broad appeal, CHIRP focused on the local community.

"That's what radio is good at. It is intimate and immediate. You can respond to things in real time in a way that you can't in a lot of other media."

Shawn doesn't view this as nostalgic but actually as a strategy. Shawn saw that commercial radio had abandoned its core strengths in pursuit of efficiency and profit. She built CHIRP around what commercial radio threw away.

The Volunteer Army That Shouldn't Work But Does

CHIRP (Chicago Independent Radio Project) breaks every business rule: it runs on volunteers. All 240 of them across 13 departments, programming live, delivering results that rival commercial stations.

"For the first five years, I wasn't getting paid, so I worked other jobs," Shawn recalls. This sacrifice during the early years built a culture of commitment that continues today.

Take Maria, a graphic designer who'd never been on the radio. She started with orientation, read the materials, and created a sample playlist mixing electronic beats with Chicago house music. After one-on-one studio training, she did three sessions with current DJs, learning how to work the board, manage dead air, and read weather updates. Six months later, she was hosting "Design Sounds," connecting music to visual art movements and drawing regular listeners who planned their Tuesday evenings around her show.

"I feel proud that I've built a culture where people take the work seriously. They're proud of it. They understand that there are high standards, and they continue to perpetuate those standards as new people come in."

Most organizations assume volunteers mean amateur quality. Shawn proved the opposite: CHIRP's coverage of Lollapalooza drew 50,000 online listeners, which was more than some commercial stations pull during drive time.

While Spotify and Apple Music bet on algorithms, Shawn bet on something radical: humans who cared about what they played.

"With all these online sources of music, discovery is easier than ever before. However, in a way, it's also harder than ever before. With human DJs in real time, curating shows, there is that personal touch."

The value is personal connection. Shawn mentioned she expects the personal touch from DJs to sound something like this: "'Here's what I think you would like to know about this song I'm going to play. Here's a little bit of background about it.' So it's not just an anonymous piece of music, but you find out a little bit about it."

While streaming services offered infinite choice, CHIRP offered informed choice.

What started as one woman's frustration with commercial radio became a national movement to restore community broadcasting. Shawn's vision extended beyond building one station to changing the entire landscape. CHIRP played a crucial role in passing the Local Community Radio Act, which "allowed for new low-power FM stations to be on the air."

"We lobbied in D.C. twice, we collected thousands of letters, then had the opportunity to lead a White House meeting." The impact was massive: "Because of the bill that we helped pass, there are more than a thousand new low-power FMs on the air across the country."

Then something unexpected happened: by focusing intensely on Chicago, CHIRP attracted listeners worldwide.

"We intentionally focus on Chicago, which people in other places just find interesting."

Shawn's model contradicts what most people assume about online content. Most creators make content faceless and placeless to appeal to everyone. "You don't want to make it too specific, because that might turn somebody off. But we are the opposite."

In Chicago, "You're guaranteed to hear at least two Chicago artists every single hour of the day on CHIRP. You'll never hear fewer than that."

CHIRP also hosts other events to introduce new artists and listen to their music.

This local focus didn't limit the radio station's reach-it expanded. CHIRP gets 40,000 weekly listeners from 67 countries, with regular listeners in Tokyo, Berlin, and São Paulo who plan their days around Chicago programming. "We have a real community of expatriate Chicagoans who listen all over the world, including a substantial audience in New Zealand."

CHIRP proves that an authentic local connection becomes the ultimate differentiator in an increasingly digital world. Don't chase universal appeal. Serve your specific community so well that others want to be part of the experience.

Building Community Infrastructure

CHIRP's community integration runs deep. When the CTA shut down the Blue Line in winter of 2024, CHIRP became the unofficial information hub, with DJs giving real-time updates between songs. They're members of five different Chambers of Commerce, promoting local businesses on-air during morning drive time. When Thalia Hall needs to fill seats for an indie band, they get a live interview spot. When the Chicago Food Bank needs volunteers, CHIRP's DJs make personal appeals that regularly bring in 200+ people for weekend shifts.

The station works with more than a hundred nonprofits annually, not just reading PSAs but creating actual partnerships. During COVID, they organized virtual fundraisers that raised $150,000 for local restaurants struggling to survive.

Shawn didn't do this by accident; it was her plan from the beginning. She saw that commercial radio had abandoned its role as a community connector. CHIRP filled that gap.

I asked Shawn about her predictions for the future based on what she's seeing: "Within the next five years, we'll see a massive backlash against algorithmic content curation. "I'm already seeing it with our younger DJs. They're telling me their friends are frustrated with

Spotify playing the same songs over and over, even on 'discovery' playlists. People are starting to realize that AI recommendations keep them in bubbles."

Increasingly, people will crave human curation that introduces them to things they would never have found on their own. "We're getting more requests for DJ recommendations than ever before. People want someone they trust to say, 'Here's something you've never heard that I think you'll love.'" The radio stations and content creators who survive will be the ones who master the art of human discovery, rather than simply giving people what they want, but giving them what they didn't know they wanted.

The most innovative thing you can do might be returning to what worked before everyone forgot why it mattered. Shawn proved that innovation can involve embracing traditional values. Her volunteer-driven model achieves professional quality by combining time-less principles with contemporary technology.

Her success in creating global reach through local authenticity proves that a genuine human connection becomes your competitive advantage in an increasingly automated world.

What Possibilities are Available to You?

Look for what your industry abandoned in pursuit of efficiency or profit. Where has your field sacrificed its core values? That's probably your opportunity.

Build systems that make people excellent, not just efficient. Treat your team or volunteers seriously, and they'll rise to meet high expectations.

Double down on authentic connection instead of chasing universal appeal. Focus on serving your specific community so well that others want to be part of the experience.

You don't need to abandon what made your field valuable in the first place. You're better off doing it better than anyone else remembers how.

Shawn built CHIRP by bringing back what commercial radio forgot: human connection and community engagement. But what happens when you take that same back-to-basics approach and apply it to an industry that's supposed to be cutting-edge? Our final chapter features pioneer, Sonat Birnecker-Hart, who discovered that sometimes the most impactful solution means helping others succeed by building the systems and methods others can use.

Chapter 13
"Who Wrote the Laws?"

"Who am I? How am I using my time to make things better for my family, my community, and the world?"

Sonat Birnecker Hart asks herself this question every Yom Kippur. It's why she and her husband, Robert, walked away from dream careers. Sonat had tenure as a German history professor, and Robert had diplomatic immunity working for the Austrian Embassy. Together, they decided to build Chicago's first distillery since the 1800s.

The problem? Illinois had no laws allowing craft distilleries to exist.

So Sonat wrote them.

The Personal Problem That Broke an Industry Open

Sonat's parents were getting older. She wanted to be closer to them. Her husband, Robert, grew up learning to make spirits from his grandfather, but he'd never run a business. They both loved Chicago.

"How do I find a way to be close to my aging parents, work with my husband, and build something together in the city I love, that's worth giving up our secure careers?"

Most people would have moved somewhere easier or stayed put. Sonat researched the problem instead.

Illinois required craft distilleries to produce 100,000 gallons annually. That's four swimming pools' worth of alcohol. The licensing fee was $100,000. No small business could survive those requirements.

Instead of accepting it, Sonat called her state senator.

Fixing Laws Instead of Working Around Them

For months, Sonat drove to Springfield, explaining why the law made no sense. Working with Senator Heather Steans and Representative Greg Harris, she helped write the Craft Distiller Act.

The new law dropped the production requirement to 2,500 gallons. Cut licensing fees to $2,500. It also allowed on-site sales and tastings for the first time since Prohibition.

Illinois went from zero craft distilleries to over 30 in five years.

When Everyone Calls, Start Teaching

Word got out about Chicago's first distillery. Sonat's phone wouldn't stop ringing.

"We read about you. How did you start a distillery?"

At first, she just answered questions for free. Then she responded: "Come to our workshop."

The cost was $3,000 per person. People flew to Chicago from six continents—3,500 students and counting.

Then Sonat discovered workshop attendees needed equipment. So she became an equipment dealer. They needed ongoing help? She started a consulting firm.

Every problem became a business.

Learning Everything the Hard Way First

Robert programmed their entire inventory system from

scratch. They write their contracts. Handle their legal work in three countries.

"When you do the work yourself, you understand the pitfalls and challenges. You see opportunities others miss."

When workshop students ask detailed questions, Sonat has real answers because she's done the work.

Teaching Distributors How to Sell

Illinois has a three-tier system. Distilleries sell to distributors, who sell to retailers. Simple, except distributors only knew big brands like Jack Daniel's.

"There wasn't understanding about craft brands. Finding people to work with us was difficult."

So Sonat taught them, too. Distributor by distributor, retailer by retailer, she explained what craft spirits were and why they mattered.

Family Values, Community Action

KOVAL honors both their grandfathers. Sonat's great-grandfather left Vienna to start a business near where their distillery stands today. Robert's grandfather taught him to distill.

When COVID hit, they converted the entire distillery to make hand sanitizer and donated it to Chicago's fire departments, police, jails, and courthouses. The city gave them the Medal of Honor.

"I don't think you just go to work and go home. Everything is you, and you're part of your community."

KOVAL spirits now sell in 44 countries. But here's the real impact: Sonat has helped set up over 200 distilleries worldwide. Remember those 3,500 workshop graduates? They went home and started distilleries in their communities.

What's Coming Next Besides AI?

"Manufacturing will continue to be incredibly important, but we don't value it enough because we don't teach it in schools."

Sonat sees the problem everywhere: hundreds of Chicago-area factories with no succession plans when owners retire. Students graduate without manufacturing skills.

AI and robotics will revolutionize everything, but small businesses aren't preparing. So she joined the boards for North Branch Works and Manufacturing Renaissance. Not to talk about solutions but to create them.

How You Can Make a Difference

Right now in your industry, there's probably a law that's outdated or flawed that everyone just accepts. Knowledge is dying with retiring experts because no one is capturing it. The infrastructure is missing because everyone's waiting for someone else to build it.

Sonat didn't set out to revolutionize American distilling. She wanted to live near her aging parents and work with her husband. That personal choice led her to rewrite state laws, teach thousands of entrepreneurs, and enable hundreds of businesses worldwide.

What broken system is blocking your path? What if you fixed it for everyone instead of working around it?

The infrastructure you build today becomes the foundation others build on tomorrow.

What's your answer to Sonat's question: "How am I using my time to make things better for my family, my community, and the world?"

Epilogue
Your Pioneer Moment

Your Pioneer Moment

You have the potential to be a pioneer at any age or stage in life. Are you tired of tolerating something that drives you crazy every single day?

That frustration? It's telling you something important. There's an opportunity waiting when you look at the problem differently.

The pioneers in this book didn't wake up planning to change the world. They woke up thinking, "Why doesn't anyone else see this?"

The Coffee Cup That Changed Everything

Tenia Davis carried two cups of coffee into what would become the most important conversation of her career.

One for herself, one for the boss who'd been systematically excluding her from meetings for months.

"I love what I'm doing," she told him that morning. "I'm pretty good at it, and I'm learning a lot from this team. I don't want to leave the team, but I need you to be the leader that I respect."

The words surprised even her. She hadn't planned to say them. But there they were, hanging in the air between two coffee cups and years of accumulated frustration.

That moment contains everything you need to know about being ahead of your time.

Four Skills Anyone Can Master

Tenia succeeded because she mastered four specific skills. You can too.

Question Everything, Especially "Common Sense"

Everyone told Tenia to keep her head down. Accept the situation. That's just how toxic bosses operate. She asked a different question: "What if this isn't about me?"

Instead of assuming she was the problem, Tenia looked at the pattern. Great employees came in motivated, then became disengaged six months later. The environment was breaking people, not the other way around.

She questioned the most fundamental assumption in business: that "problem employees" are the problem.

Ground Your Vision in Evidence

Tenia didn't walk into that coffee meeting with feelings and complaints. She brought printed research. Her supervisor's bio, highlighted in yellow with the skills she wanted to learn. Specific examples of how she'd been excluded. Clear requests for what she needed.

"You're brilliant. You're smart. That's why I'm here. I want to learn from you. But you're not creating a way for me to learn from you."

Facts opened doors that emotions couldn't budge.

Find the Side Doors

When her direct supervisor failed her, Tenia built relationships with other leaders throughout the organization who could teach her what she needed to know. She didn't play the game everyone else was playing. She created her own game with better rules.

Act Before You're Ready

That conversation could have ended Tenia's career. Her supervisor could have fired her or made her life worse. She spoke up anyway because she realized something profound: staying in a broken system that didn't let her thrive served no one.

Sometimes the most professional thing you can do is refuse to accept conditions that diminish you.

Your Coffee Cup Moment Is Waiting

Right now, you're probably tolerating something that keeps eating at you. A policy that makes no sense. A process that wastes everyone's time. A problem everyone complains about but no one fixes.

That frustration? That's your pioneer signal.

Here's what I want you to know: You're not imagining it. You're not being too sensitive. If something feels broken to you, it probably is. And you probably already know how to fix it.

The problems driving you crazy are driving everyone else crazy too. They're just pretending it's fine because they don't think they can change anything.

But you can.

The Ripple Effect

Tenia's coffee cup courage didn't just solve her problem. It showed her that most workplace dysfunction isn't about bad people—it's about bad systems. That insight now guides how she helps organizations create environments where everyone can do their best work.

Her courage rippled outward. When Tenia spoke up, three other people in her department started having their own difficult conversations. The leaders she works with today create better conditions for their teams. People she mentors know they don't have to accept toxic environments.

What You Already Have

You don't need another degree. You don't need five more years of experience. You don't need someone to tap you on the shoulder and say, "Okay, now you can be a pioneer."

Every pioneer in this book started with what they already knew. Sonat had her academic research skills. Andy had his marketing experience. Tenia had her ability to see patterns and ask better questions.

That thing you've been doing for years that seems boring to you? Someone needs exactly that expertise. The problem you solve every day without thinking? There's an entire industry that doesn't know your method exists.

Three Choices

Right now, you see something others miss. You know what I'm talking about. That thing that makes you want to bang your head against the wall every day.

You have three choices:

1 Keep quiet and stay comfortable

2 Complain and stay stuck

3 Fix it yourself

The pioneers in this book chose option three. Not because they were special, but because they couldn't stand options one and two anymore.

Your 20-Minute Conversation

Tenia's conversation lasted 20 minutes. It changed her career and the careers of everyone she's mentored since.

What 20-minute conversation are you avoiding? What broken system exhausts you every day? What obvious solution does everyone dismiss as impossible?

You already know the answers. You've known them for a while now.

I'm Going to Tell You Something True

That frustration you feel isn't a character flaw. It's intelligence. You're not crazy for thinking there's a better way. You're just the first one brave enough to admit the current way doesn't work.

Your frustration is trying to tell you something important: You see solutions others can't see yet. You spot problems others have learned to ignore. You have the ability to fix something that's been broken for too long.

The question isn't whether you're qualified. The question is whether you'll still be complaining about this exact problem next year, or whether you'll be the reason it doesn't exist anymore.

Your Move

Every single thing that makes your life better exists because someone, somewhere, said, "This doesn't work. I'm going to fix it."

Now it's your turn.

What will you fix? What will you build? What will you refuse to accept for one more day?

The pioneer in you already knows. You've been carrying those two coffee cups for months, maybe years. One for you, one for the conversation that changes everything.

This isn't new. People have been having coffee cup conversations that change the world for centuries. The question isn't whether you'll act. It's when.

Make it today. I'll be cheering you on.

About the Author

Lynn Miller has always been drawn to the questions no one else asks.

This isn't random curiosity. The questions Lynn asks pioneers turn their ahead-of-their-time insights into movements that matter.

Lynn's journey to becoming a pioneer whisperer took an unconventional path. Her discipline as a classically trained singer taught her that excellence comes from repetition, but innovation comes from interpretation. A decade at a billion-dollar retail organization showed her the gap between what corporate training promised and what actually changed behavior. Years of generating over $1 million annually selling online learning solutions to Fortune 500 companies revealed why most expensive programs fail: they answer questions nobody's actually asking.

Working with learning rebel Roger Schank's team at Socratic Arts changed everything. Lynn discovered that effective learning happens when people experience consequences, not consume information. She took that insight and founded Women in Growth Stage Tech, helping female tech founders address the real obstacles they faced, not the ones everyone assumed they had.

Today, as Chief Facilitator at Lynn Miller Strategies and Coordinator of Targeted Research at Networlding Publishing, Lynn helps experts escape what she calls "the curse of knowing too much." She doesn't give them templates. She asks them questions that make them squirm until they find the words that make people lean in instead of tune out.

Ahead of Their Time emerged from Lynn's fascination with people who create new systems for broken processes instead of complaining about them. Through conversations with thirteen modern pioneers, she identified a pattern: pioneers don't predict the future. They fix the present in ways that create a **different** future.

Lynn helps people whose ideas are too early become right on time. Because being ahead of your time isn't about having all the answers-it's about asking better questions than anyone else.

In her free time, Lynn sings in the Kol Zimrah Jewish Community Choir, plays Pickleball, and visits her two grandsons as often as possible.

With Gratitude

Writing and completing this book happened because early on, I knew I couldn't do it alone. So, with the support of fiercely supportive friends and colleagues, networking support circles like The Skokie Illinois Chamber of Commerce PPN group, who kept me accountable, family, and mentors, thank you for your ongoing support.

To my networking colleague Larry Kaufman, who urged me to reconnect with Melissa G. Wilson, President of Networlding Publishing, who loves authors as much or more than I do.

My dear friend, mentor, and colleague, Melissa G. Wilson, who saw something in me that I completely overlooked, coached me through what began as a terrifying process and patiently walked me through every last challenging step I needed to take to bring this book into the world.

I appreciate you and am grateful for keeping me grounded, curious, playful, and helping me make the connections that inspired this project, as only the first of many.

To my beta readers, and listeners who helped me ensure this book resonates with the reader and offers valuable advice.

To Mila Book Covers, whose patience resulted in such a great book cover.

To Jane Wilson, who did a great job creating a landing page/website for the book.

To the early pioneers in HR Tech who shared your stories, struggles, and triumphs, thank you for allowing my curiosity to spill out onto LinkedIn posts and newsletters before I leaped into book pages.

To the thought leaders and pioneers I've worked with who wrote your books while keeping your consulting practices alive and thriving, you inspired me to keep focused on the"why" that kept pushing me forward so that I completed this first "solo" book.

To my mother, husband, children, and extended family, thank you for cheering me on and for helping me keep my father's legacy, a blessing, close to my heart during this writing process.

To my closest girlfriends since childhood, high school, and early parenthood, thank you for reminding me that writing this book was crucial to taking care of myself, even when I was too overwhelmed to find the right words.

To all the modern-day pioneers included in this book, those I interviewed who may be part of future books and past conferences, and those who aspire to be ahead of your time, thank you for your willingness to share stories that will continue to inspire me.

Before You Go

Before you go, I'd like to request a bit more of your time. If this book sparked action or if you've started questioning, building, or fixing, please write a short review on Amazon here:

https://www.amazon.com/review/create-review

Even if you read one or two chapters, you could mention why you found one specific pioneer's story more interesting and what lessons you learned.

Pioneers work better together. Share your story and find others who see what you see by emailing me at lynn@straighttalkwriter.com. The future is too important to build alone.

www.ingramcontent.com/pod-product-compliance
Lightning Source LLC
Chambersburg PA
CBHW071425210326
41597CB00020B/3651